Thurman Thomas

SPORTS REPORTS

Thurman Thomas
Star Running Back

040125

Jeff Savage

ENSLOW PUBLISHERS, INC.

Bloy St. & Ramsey Ave.   P.O. Box 38
Box 777   Aldershot
Hillside, N.J. 07205   Hants GU12 6BP
U.S.A.   U.K.

Library of Congress Cataloging-in-Publication Data

Savage, Jeff, 1961–
    Thurman Thomas: star running back / Jeff Savage.
       p. cm. — (Sports reports)
    Includes bibliographical references and index.
    Summary: A biography of running back Thurman Thomas, focusing largely on his career with the Buffalo Bills.
    ISBN 0-89490-445-0
    1. Thomas, Thurman, 1966– —Juvenile literature. 2. Football players—United States—Biography—Juvenile literature. 3. Running backs (Football)—United States—Biography—Juvenile literature. 4. Buffalo Bills (Football team)—Juvenile literature. [1. Thomas, Thurman, 1966– . 2. Football players. 3. Afro-Americans—Biography.] I. Title. II. Title: Thurman Thomas, star running back. III. Series.
GV939.T47S28 1994
796.332'092—dc20   93-2557
                                                 CIP
                                                 AC

Printed in the United States of America

10 9 8 7 6 5 4 3 2 1

Photo Credits: Terlisha A. Cockrell, pp. 23, 25, 38, 41, 42, 45; Michael Groll, Photographer, pp. 10, 14, 17, 20, 31, 62, 67, 73, 74, 83, 85, 91, 94; Sports Information Department, Oklahoma State University, pp. 49, 50, 54, 57.

Cover Photo: Michael Groll.

Contents

Chapter 1

Super Bowl

On a warm January day in Tampa, Florida, Thurman Thomas and his Buffalo Bills teammates stood on the field of Tampa Stadium doing their pregame exercises. They placed their hands on their hips, tilted their heads back and forth, and leaned from side to side. Thurman tried to concentrate, but he couldn't help thinking about where he was. The Buffalo running back looked around, and everything was so colorful: the freshly painted "Bills" logo in one end zone and "Giants" in the other; the well-groomed field of green grass; the bright blue sky; the thousands of fans entering the stadium. Thurman could feel a buzz in the air, an electricity that he had never felt before at a football game. There was a special excitement about this game, and Thurman knew it. This was the Super Bowl. Thurman had always dreamed of this day.

FACT

Among Thurman's honors in his spectacular season of 1991 was the Jim Thorpe Award which goes to the best football player of that year. Thurman was only the third running back in 12 years to win the award:

YEAR	PLAYER	TEAM	POSITION
1981	Ken Anderson	Bengals	Quarterback
1982	Dan Fouts	Chargers	Quarterback
1983	Joe Theismann	Redskins	Quarterback
1984	Dan Marino	Dolphins	Quarterback
1985	Walter Payton	Bears	Running Back
1986	Phil Simms	Giants	Quarterback
1987	Jerry Rice	49ers	Wide Receiver
1988	Roger Craig	49ers	Running Back
1989	Joe Montana	49ers	Quarterback
1990	Warren Moon	Oilers	Quarterback
1991	THURMAN THOMAS	Bills	Running Back
1992	Steve Young	49ers	Quarterback

Thurman had enjoyed success in a football uniform since he was a boy. His high school team won a state championship. His college team went to three bowl games in four years. His professional team had won the AFC Eastern Division title and qualified for the playoffs all three of his years there. Never before in the history of the Bills, though, had the team from Buffalo gone this far in the playoffs. This was the first time the Bills had made it to "The Show."

Thurman couldn't wait for the game to start. The Buffalo offense was a high-powered, quick-scoring machine that hadn't been stopped all year, and Thurman was the star running back. Millions of people from over 60 countries around the world would be watching the game on television. Thurman knew this was his chance to show everyone how great he was. Even though he led the NFL in total yards rushing and receiving combined the last two seasons, he still didn't think he was getting the respect he deserved. "I want to go out and show a lot of media guys I'm underrated and I don't get the credit that I think I deserve," Thurman said a few days before the game. "Nobody around the league, or in other cities, thinks I'm a good football player." [1]

Proving himself would not be easy. The Bills

Thurman gets ready on the scrimmage line. They wait for Kelly's signals, since they use a no-huddle offense.

had won their two playoff games with their offense—beating the Miami Dolphins 44–34 and hammering the Los Angeles Raiders 51–3. The New York Giants had won their two games mostly with defense—shutting down the Chicago Bears 31–3 and edging the San Francisco 49ers 15–13. Moving the football against the Giants would be difficult.

The Bills had already played the Giants once during the season. They had gone to Giants Stadium late in the year and triumphed by a 17–13 score. Thurman knew revenge would be on the minds of the Giants.

The sky grew dark, the stadium lights came on, and the game began with the Giants moving the ball down the field. Jeff Hostetler completed passes to Howard Cross and Mark Ingram, bringing the ball to the Bills' 15-yard line, and the Giants threatened to score first. Hostetler was the quarterback for the Giants because their regular starting quarterback, Phil Simms, had been injured in the previous loss to the Bills. Giants' running back Ottis Anderson ran the ball twice to reach the 11, and Matt Bahr kicked a field goal from there to give New York a 3–0 lead.

Now it was the Bills' turn. The offense ran onto the field, and the first play called in the huddle was for Thurman. He took the handoff and ran up the middle, but got crunched after just a two-yard gain. This was going to be a tough game. A few plays later, Jim Kelly threw a pass downfield to James Lofton. The Giants' defensive back Perry Williams tipped the ball up in the air, but Lofton grabbed it and raced down the sideline until he was caught at the eight-yard line. Now it was the Bills who were threatening. After an incomplete pass, Thurman ran three yards to the five. On third down, Kelly threw a pass to Thomas in the left corner of the end zone, but Thomas was triple-teamed, and the pass was batted away. Scott Norwood kicked a short field goal to tie the score, 3–3.

On Buffalo's next possession, Thurman ran for three more yards up the middle, and then Andre Reed caught three straight passes to get past midfield. Thurman ran six yards through the middle to the 41-yard line, and the first quarter ended with the Bills on the move.

Thurman is five feet, ten inches and 197 pounds, which is considered small for a running back, but he is quick and elusive. He showed his speed on the first play of the second quarter when Kelly lobbed a short pass to him. He darted 13 yards to the Giants' 28, where linebacker Carl Banks slammed him to the turf. "Thurman Thomas is just so dangerous in the open field,"[2] ABC commentator

Dan Dierdorf said on television. Thurman, though, was having trouble getting back on his feet. The force of Banks's tackle hurt Thurman, and he had to be helped from the field. TV announcer Al Michaels said, "The sight of Thomas going off the field would put a lump in any Buffalo fan's throat."[3] Thurman only missed one play. He got back in the game in time to help his team reach the one-yard line, where substitute running back Don Smith crashed into the end zone to give the Bills a 9–3 lead. The extra point was kicked, and the score was 10–3.

The Bills' defense came up with the game's next big play when Hostetler dropped back to pass and stumbled over Anderson's foot in the end zone. As Hostetler rose to his feet, big defensive end Bruce Smith pulled him back down for a safety. Buffalo now led, 12–3, and everything was going according to plan.

The Giants didn't give up and drove all the way down the field. From the 14-yard line, Hostetler threw a perfect pass to Stephen Baker in the end zone on third down for a touchdown with 25 seconds left before the half. At halftime, the Bills' lead was down to two points, 12–10.

The Bills had talked all season of getting to "The Show." Two years before, when Thurman was a

Jim Kelly has lead the Buffalo Bills to three consecutive Super Bowls—XXV, XXVI, XXVII.

rookie, they had fought among themselves about who was in charge of the team, and they became known as the "Bickering Bills." It's no wonder they lost that year in the playoffs. The next year, they lost a heartbreaking game in the first round of the playoffs at Cleveland when running back Ronnie Harmon dropped the winning pass in the end zone. After that game, the Bills vowed to get to the Super Bowl. Now that they were here, in Tampa Stadium against the Giants, they wanted more. They wanted to win it. The Giants already had won the Super Bowl three years earlier. The Bills said in the locker room at halftime that it was their turn.

The Giants got the ball to start the second half, and they went on the longest time-consuming drive in Super Bowl history. They kept the ball for almost nine-and-a-half minutes as they drove from their 20-yard line down the field toward the end zone. Thurman stood on the sideline, wishing his team could somehow get the ball back. The Giants reached the one-yard line, where Anderson burst over the line for a touchdown. With less than six minutes left in the third quarter, the Giants had their first lead of the game, 17–12.

The Bills couldn't move the ball on their next possession, but neither could the Giants, and the Bills got the ball back with one minute left in the third quarter. They moved downfield and on the last play of the quarter, Kelly threw a dump-off pass to Thurman. The quick running back juked past Banks and spun past two more defenders for a nine-yard gain to the Giants' 31-yard line. Thurman knew his team needed to score on this drive, and as he walked to the other end of the field with his teammates to begin the final quarter, he talked about how he had to make a big play.

In the huddle to begin the fourth quarter, Kelly called for a handoff to Thomas. Thurman pulled the ball into his stomach and started downfield. He reached the 25-yard line, where he broke through the tackle of linebacker Gary Reasons. He jumped to his right and darted forward three more yards, where safety Myron Guyton was waiting. Thurman lowered his head and bounced off Guyton. Then he slipped past cornerback Reyna Thompson at the 20. He cut to the right sideline, then sprinted downfield, past linebacker Lawrence Taylor, and into the end zone for a spectacular touchdown. It was the longest run of the game, and the score gave the Bills the lead, 18–17. Kicker Scott Norwood made the extra point, and the Bills led by two, 19–17. Thurman was mobbed by his teammates in the end zone after coming up with the big play the team needed.

The Giants, however, weren't through. Hostetler moved his side smartly down the field, and Anderson made some key runs to get the ball in field-goal position for Bahr, who kicked it through the uprights with seven minutes left. The Giants led again, 20–19.

The Bills needed a field goal to win it. Thurman did his best to get his team in position by gaining four yards on a sweep and then dodging his way for 15 more on a pass. The Bills couldn't move any further and were forced to punt. Now, it was up to the defense. Thurman waited on the sideline knowing if his offense could just get one more chance, the Bills could score. Sure enough, the Bills' defense stopped the Giants at midfield, and they punted to the Buffalo 10-yard line with just over two minutes left in the game. This would be Buffalo's last chance.

Kelly gained nine yards on two quarterback scrambles, and it was third and one from the 19. The Bills hadn't made a third-down conversion in the game and needed one here. Kelly called the play for Thomas. Thurman took the handoff and cut left, away from a huge pile. He ducked past two defenders and, suddenly, was out in the open. He ran as fast as he could down the field until he was tripped by Giants' cornerback Everson Walls at the

Thomas guards the ball as he follows his blocker downfield.

40-yard line. ABC commentator Frank Gifford announced, "What a show Thurman Thomas is putting on tonight."[4]

There was just one minute to go, and the clock was moving. Kelly passed five yards to Reed to the 45, then ran nine yards, across midfield, to the Giants' 46, where Buffalo called its last time out with 48 seconds left.

The closest Super Bowl ever was 19 years earlier when the Baltimore Colts defeated the Dallas Cowboys, 16–13, on a last-second field goal in Super Bowl V. Would the Bills win this game in the last second? One thing was certain. Most people already were calling it the most exciting Super Bowl ever.

The Bills' offense came back on the field following the time-out. On the first play, Kelly dropped back and threw a pass to tight end Keith McKeller, who bent down to catch the ball at his feet at the 40-yard line, where he was tackled. The clock was running . . . 37 seconds . . . 36 . . . 35 . . . 34 . . . Kelly handed off to Thurman, who flowed to his right and somehow slipped through the grasp of Banks and Taylor and broke free up the middle. He was caught and tackled by cornerback Mark Collins, but not before picking up 11 yards and putting the Bills in field-goal position at the 29-yard line. Kicker Scott Norwood sprinted on the field. Only eight seconds were left on the clock. The Giants called a time-out to try to make the kicker more nervous. The crowd buzzed with excitement. The Giants waved their arms in the air to distract the Bills. The Buffalo players and coaches held hands on the sideline. Norwood lined up the field goal. It would be a 47-yarder, just at the edge of his range. He knew he couldn't kick it any farther. The snap was good. The ball was spotted. Norwood thrust his right foot forward and kicked the ball. It sailed skyward. Players from both teams stood on the field and watched the flight of the ball. It headed for the right upright. Would it go through or miss wide? Would the Bills or the Giants win? The ball reached the upright and . . . went wide to the right. No good. The Giants won the game.

The Giants bounced around on the field like jumping beans. They celebrated the wildest Super Bowl finish in history. Meanwhile, the Bills stood in disbelief. Thurman just stared at the ground. His team had come so close. It was the narrowest margin of defeat in a Super Bowl ever. Nothing could hurt more than this loss.

Afterward, Norwood said, "I'm sure I'll never forget it. It's something I'll carry with me."[5] Thurman, however, did not blame his team's kicker for the loss. "It shouldn't have come down to that kick in the first place,"[6] Thurman said.

Giants' linebacker Lawrence Taylor said that the defense keyed on Thomas. "We tried to take Thurman out of the passing game because he is the key to it," Taylor said. "Of course, that's going to hurt us when it comes to him running the ball."[7]

Thomas accounted for over half of Buffalo's offense by rushing 15 times for 135 yards and catching five passes for 55 more. Still, the Super Bowl MVP is traditionally awarded to a player from the winning team, and New York running back Ottis Anderson received the honor by rushing for

Thurman Thomas is well liked by his teammates.

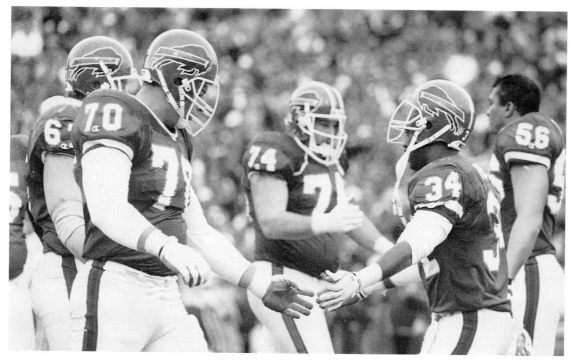

102 yards and catching one pass. Thurman told reporters that not winning the MVP didn't bother him. "We didn't win the ball game, so you have to say that somebody on their team deserved to be the most valuable player," he said. "If we would have won, maybe it would have been different."[8]

Quarterback Jim Kelly was furious that Thurman was overlooked. "Who was the best running back on the field?" Kelly responded to reporters. "Pardon me. You didn't see Thurman Thomas?"[9]

The Bills lost the game, and Thurman didn't get the MVP trophy. That's how it will always read in the record books, anyway. Thurman did something, though, that he always wanted to do. He showed sports fans around the world just how great he was. He also knew he would get his chance again.

Chapter 2

Missouri City, Texas

"I don't want to go, Mamma!"[1] Thurman shouted as he ran to his room. His mother, Terlisha, followed him into the bedroom and told him he had to go to his cousins' house for the family dinner.

Thurman grew up in Missouri City, Texas, just outside of Houston where he was born on May 16, 1966. When he was three years old, his mother and his father were divorced. Both of his parents soon remarried, and instead of having just two adults watching over him, Thurman now had four. He lived with his mother, Terlisha, and stepfather, Gilbert, but he also spent a lot of time with his father, also named Thurman, and his stepmother, Ann, who lived nearby. Thurman didn't have any brothers or sisters, but he had nine cousins. All of them were girls. By the time Thurman reached the second grade, he realized how much he didn't like playing with girls.

Thurman sat on his stuffed animal bull in the corner of his room. "But Mamma," he said with a sad face, "girls are no fun. They can't play baseball. They can't play football. They can't do anything fun."[2] Thurman's mother insisted that her son go to the family dinner. So Thurman took with him his yellow Tonka truck. When he got to his cousins' house, he played alone in the backyard. Thurman's idea of real fun was sports. It didn't matter to him whether it was baseball or football or basketball, just as long as it didn't include girls.

Thurman grew up an only child. For the first few years of his life, his only playmates were his cousins.

When Thurman was seven, he joined a Little League baseball team. After the coach saw how well Thurman could throw and catch, he said, "Son, you can play any position you like."[3] Thurman was a pitcher and an outfielder. Thurman could hit well even though his bat was almost as tall as he was. What Thurman did best of all, though, was run. He was the fastest player on his team, and almost every time he reached first base, he stole second and third. After three years of playing on the baseball team, Thurman's parents decided it was time to let him join a Pop Warner football team.

Thurman had been preparing for football. His father was a running back at Prairie View A&M,

and his uncle, Grady Cavness, played cornerback for the Atlanta Falcons and Denver Broncos. Thurman's father often came to the house, and since Uncle Grady lived right across the street, the two of them would teach Thurman everything they knew about the game. Thurman's friends would come over, and they'd play tackle football on Roberson Street, out in front of Thurman's house. Thurman's father and uncle would watch from the sidewalk. When it got too dark to see, the game would end. Thurman would go into the house and sit down in the living room, where his father and uncle would tell him what he did right and wrong that day. When Thurman joined the Pop Warner Colts, he was ready.

Thurman played tailback and became a star. He could jump around and make the defenders miss him, or he could run right past them. He scored the most touchdowns on the team and fell in love with football. He couldn't wait to play for his school. The following year, Thurman entered Missouri City Junior High School and immediately signed up for the football team. He was crushed to learn that, as a sixth grader, he had to wait a year to play. Only the bigger seventh and eighth graders could play for Missouri City Junior High. So Thurman had to watch the games from the

*As Thurman grew older, he longed to play with other boys. Around
this time, he began learning about football from his father and uncle.*

stands that year. He paid close attention to the running backs and often said: "I can do better than that. If that were me, I would've made that touchdown."[4]

The following year, when Thurman entered the seventh grade, he was issued a helmet and a set of shoulder pads as a member of the Missouri City Junior High football team. The coach had heard how good Thurman was and named him the team's starting tailback without even seeing him play. Thurman proved to be better than even the coach had expected, leading his team in rushing both years. He had a great ability to fake out defenders, and he was strong enough to drag tacklers with him. His nickname was "Bull" because his mother says he was big as a baby, but his teammates called him "Bull" because he was so tough. Thurman was also developing a very competitive attitude. He hated to lose. When his team lost a game, which wasn't often, he wouldn't talk to anyone. He would walk home, go straight to his room, close the door, and either listen to music or just lie on his bed and stare at the ceiling. He usually would not talk to anyone until the next day.

When an important decision had to be made involving Thurman, his father and mother and their spouses would gather in the living room and discuss the situation with the boy. They called these meetings "conferences." One time, when Thurman was 12, the family called a "conference" because Thurman had done something bad. He had called his mother at work and asked if he could go out for the afternoon with some friends. When she told him she wanted him to stay home that day, Thurman hung up the phone and got so mad that he kicked a hole in the wall. He pushed a potted plant in front of the hole to try and hide it, but when his mother came home, she saw the plant in front of the wall and knew it didn't belong there. When she moved the plant, she found the hole in the wall. It was decided at the conference that Thurman would be placed on restriction. He wasn't allowed to use the telephone or watch television or go outside for two weeks. Thurman behaved much better after that.

As Thurman got older, he couldn't stop thinking about football. He really wanted to impress his family, especially his father and uncle, who had taught him how to play. When his team lost, he never blamed anyone else. He always felt that he should have done better. Thurman was happy just to be playing. He remembered not being allowed to play football as a sixth grader, when he had to sit in the stands and watch the games. He never wanted to experience something like that again. Little did he know that was exactly what was about to happen—again.

When Thurman enrolled at Willowridge High School, all he could think of was playing football. Willowridge was coming off an average season, and Thurman figured the team could use a good running back. Thurman knew he was the man for the job. Neal Quinlan, the coach, was excited to have a boy as talented as Thurman at his school, but he had to give him some bad news. Freshmen were not allowed to play on the varsity team. Thurman was heartbroken. The coach really wanted the talented runner to play on the varsity squad, and he asked the school administrators if there was some way to bend the rule. It was no use. Thurman had to play his first year with the freshman Eagles. As expected, he was the star. He played tailback on offense and cornerback on defense, the same positions his father and uncle played during their football careers.

Midway through the freshman season, Thurman learned a valuable lesson. He decided one day that he did not feel like going to practice. He walked past the field after school and went home instead. He thought that because he was the star, he didn't have to practice every day like the other players. Besides, he figured he should be playing for the varsity team, anyway. When he returned to practice the following day, he found out he was in trouble. The coaches told him he wouldn't be allowed to play in the upcoming game. At first, Thurman was angry at the coaches. Eventually, though, he realized that he had only himself to blame. He understood that even though he was more talented than the other players on the team, he did not deserve special privileges. He realized the true meaning of a "team" sport. The Eagles played the next game without Thurman and lost. Now Thurman felt even worse. He had let the team down. The coaches hoped Thurman had learned his lesson. It was the only loss the freshman Eagles suffered all season. They finished with a 9-1 record.

Thurman would watch the varsity games on Friday nights and pretend he was the running back, with all the fans in the bleachers cheering for him. He could hardly wait until his sophomore year when he would be playing with the big team.

Chapter 3

High School Hero

Thurman's hero was the Houston Oilers' running back Earl Campbell, who wore jersey number 34. When Thurman showed up for the first day of football practice in his sophomore year, he asked Coach Quinlan for number 34. The coach gave it to him with a smile. Thurman came running out onto the field wearing his new uniform and his teammates nicknamed him "Yoda" after the Star Wars character because Thurman's helmet fit over his head in an odd manner. Thurman didn't mind the new nickname; he just wanted to play.

The newspapers predicted Willowridge High would finish somewhere in the middle of the league. The sportswriters knew very little about the football team because the school was only two years old, and this was just the second year of varsity competition. The sportswriters knew even

Since high school, Thurman has worn 34 on his jersey—the same number as his hero, Earl Campbell.

less about Thurman Thomas. That situation would soon change.

Rodney Brown was the quarterback for the Eagles, and he wore jersey number 1. Tailback Ron Garner wore number 14, wingback Terry Rose wore number 44 and Thurman, who played fullback, wore number 34. These were the four stars of the team and the newspapers were soon calling them "Ace and the Three Fours." Thomas was on the field for every down, whether it was offense, defense, or special teams. He was the holder on field goals and extra points. One of the "special" types of plays he often made was on extra points. Thurman would take the snap from center. If he noticed that the defensive players were not taking the correct angle on the rush, he would take off with the ball around the end for the two-point conversion.

The Eagles rolled through the regular season undefeated to win the league title and reach the playoffs. Thurman also played cornerback, and his big defensive play gave the Eagles a miracle victory in the playoffs. The Eagles were playing mighty Beaumont Hebert High, another team that had gone unbeaten through the season and had won its previous playoff game, 50–7. Beaumont's star player was fullback Jerry Ball, who now plays noseguard for the Detroit Lions. The newspapers said that Beaumont was a three-touchdown favorite in the game. Even the students at Willowridge High didn't think their team had a chance. They sat quietly during the pep rally on campus the day of the game, and some of the teachers even yelled cheers for Beaumont High, a school that had a great football tradition in the Houston area.

Seven thousand fans attended the game at Pasadena Memorial Stadium in southeast Houston and watched Beaumont take a 7–6 lead at halftime. Midway through the third quarter, Ball rumbled through the defense 50 yards for a touchdown, and when the conversion was made, Beaumont was ahead, 14–6. Willowridge answered with a touchdown of its own to make it 14–12 early in the fourth quarter. The Eagles tried a two-point conversion to tie the game, but failed. The Eagles' defense stopped Beaumont to give the offense one more chance to win it with time running down. Thurman and his teammates drove the length of the field to get in position to kick a field goal. With three minutes left, John Simpson kicked the 20-yarder to give the Eagles a 15–14 lead. Without much time, Beaumont came right back. Quarterback Gerald Landry completed pass after pass, and suddenly

FACT

Thurman Thomas helped the Willowridge High School Eagles become one of the top football teams in Texas. Among his achievements while in high school, Thomas led his team to the Texas State Championship in his junior year. He was honored later as the best offensive high school player in the state for the entire decade of the 1980s.

Beaumont was at the Eagles' 15-yard line with a minute left. Landry dropped back and threw a pass into the corner of the end zone toward Thurman's side. Thurman ran toward the receiver and jumped in front of him to intercept the pass and win the game.

"We could always count on Thurman to come up with a special play to win the game,"[1] Coach Quinlan said.

The Eagles lost in the playoffs the following week to Brownwood High and their famous coach, Gordon Wood, who has more victories than any other high school coach in the country. Still, it was a very satisfying year for the Eagles who finished 9–1 and proved they were as good as any team in the Houston area.

The following season everyone expected big things from junior fullback Thurman Thomas and Willowridge High. Thurman and his teammates delivered. The team sailed through the regular season unbeaten to reach the playoffs once again. In the sixth game of the season, against tough rival A&M Consolidated at Kyle Field, home of Texas A&M University, Thurman returned a punt 80 yards to give the Eagles a 13–0 lead. On the ensuing kickoff, Thurman crashed into a teammate and suffered a broken nose. He went to the sideline with blood pouring from his nose and sat down on the bench and tilted his head back. He wanted to get right back into the game, but his nose wouldn't stop bleeding. A&M Consolidated drove down the field and scored a touchdown to cut the lead to 13–7 while Thurman sat on the bench with a towel over his nose. Finally, he got back into the game and helped keep A&M from scoring again as Willowridge held on.

In the seventh game against Brenham High, Thurman returned the opening kickoff for a touchdown, and his team went on to win, 41–0. The following week was the big showdown for the district championship against crosstown rival Tomball High. It was billed as a match-up between Thurman and Tomball's running back Roger Vick, who went on to play for the New York Jets. On Tomball's first possession, Vick broke up the middle and went all the way for a 60-yard touchdown. Willowridge came right back on its first play when Thurman took a handoff, cut left, then back to the right, and sprinted down the sideline 65 yards for a tying touchdown. Tomball came back to take a 9–7 lead, but the Eagles took control of the game from that point and won, 39–9.

Thurman and his teammates agreed that they were a better team than the year before and that they were good enough to make it to the state championship. They would have to win four straight games in the playoffs to get there. In the opening game, they beat Austin Westlake, 34–0. In the second round, they beat Jasper, 34–7. In the third game, they beat Bay City, 34–12. Thurman knew then this was a special year because in all three playoff games the Eagles scored exactly 34 points—his jersey number.

The state semifinal game was held in the Houston Astrodome, and 11,000 fans came to see Willowridge High play New Braunfels High. Thurman was excited to be playing in the same stadium where Earl Campbell plays for the Oilers, but he was also quite upset. The Willowridge offense was getting a lot of recognition because of its explosiveness, but Thurman felt that the defense was being overlooked. The Eagles, with Thurman playing cornerback, had allowed only three touchdowns in three playoff games. Against New Braunfels, Willowridge took a 7–0 lead after a long drive down the field. Then, the defense forced New Braunfels to punt, and Thurman fielded it at his 25-yard line. He broke up the middle, outmaneuvered four defenders, and raced down the left sideline 75 yards for a touchdown. Willowridge went on to an easy 38–0 victory. The Eagles had made it to the Texas Class 4A championship game.

The Texas title game was played at Kyle Field in mid-December, and over 12,000 fans showed up to see Willowridge take on mighty Corsicana High. The Eagles were small in size compared to the Corsicana players, who weighed about 30 pounds more per player. Willowridge countered with the quickness of "Ace and the Three Fours." The teams were tied 10–10 at the half. In the locker room, Thurman stood up and said to his teammates: "You can do better than this. We didn't come here to lose. Don't think the team we're playing against isn't good. We have to play better."[2]

Willowridge scored the only touchdown of the third quarter to take a 16–10 lead, and the game grew tense as the fourth quarter arrived. Everyone at Willowridge knew the team had to play one more good quarter to win the state championship. Late in the fourth quarter, the Eagles had the ball with a third down at their own 40-yard line. They knew they had to get a first down or else give the ball back to the dangerous Corsicana offense. In the huddle, quarterback Rodney Brown called for a pitchout to tailback Ron Garner. On the play, the Corsicana strong safety blitzed. He headed directly for Garner, but at the last moment Thurman jumped in the way to make the block and spring Garner free to run down the sideline for a 60-yard touchdown and a 22–10 lead. The Eagles' sideline erupted, but it was too early to celebrate. A two-point conversion attempt failed. Corsicana drove back down the field for a touchdown to make it 22–17. Corsicana tried an onside kick. Willowridge recovered. The Eagles ran out the clock. When the gun sounded to signal the end of the game, the Willowridge students poured onto the field in one of the wildest celebrations ever in the Astrodome. Thurman rolled around on the field with his teammates as they celebrated a perfect 13-0 season. He had rushed for 122 yards in the game and made the key block that gave his team the winning touchdown. He finished the season with over 1,800 yards rushing and was named to the all-state team and

Thurman, with both sets of parents, deciding on what college he would attend. From left to right are: Thurman Thomas, Sr., stepmother Mary Thomas, Thurman, Terlisha Cockrell (mother), and stepfather Gilbert Cockrell.

then received the highest honor possible by being chosen as the Player of the Year by the Houston Touchdown Club.

As much as football meant to Thurman, his parents knew that he wouldn't fulfill his dream of playing college football if he didn't get good grades. Thurman paid attention in the classroom and performed well in every subject except math. So midway through Thurman's junior year at Willowridge, the family gathered in the living room and held a conference. They decided to get Thurman a tutor. It was a smart decision. The tutor helped Thurman with his homework, and he passed his math class.

Thurman's senior year was nearly as successful even though he had to overcome several obstacles. First, he suffered a sprained ankle on a kickoff in the second game of the year and had to miss the next three games. Also, it was difficult focusing on the games with all the attention he was getting. TV stations and sportswriters were often at the Willowridge practices to watch Thurman. It got to the point that he sometimes tried to avoid them. He would tell Coach Quinlan: "Hey, coach, our other players need the opportunity to talk to the press. Would you tell them I don't want to do any interviews today. Let some of the other players get some of the attention they deserve."[3]

College recruiters were a distraction as well. They showed up on campus and made so many calls to Thurman's home that he had to get a separate phone line put in his room to handle all the calls.

Thurman still helped lead the Eagles to the playoffs, and they reached the third round before losing to Bay City, one of the teams they had beaten the previous year.

Thurman immediately began focusing on college. He had joined the track team in his junior year to improve his speed by competing in the sprint events. He discussed different universities with his family. He maintained a good grade-point average so he would be able to play his freshman year. That was what he wanted most of all: to play football his freshman year.

Dozens of colleges wanted Thurman to come to their school, but the choice eventually was narrowed to three: Texas A&M, Oklahoma State, and Texas. It was a difficult decision. The University of Texas was the pride of the state, and the thought of playing for the Longhorns excited Thurman. The coaches at Texas kept talking about making Thurman a defensive back, though, and

Thurman didn't like hearing that. He was a terrific cornerback at Willowridge, but what he really wanted to do was run the ball. Texas A&M had a solid program, and Thurman liked the fact that he had already played several times at Kyle Field, home of the Aggies. The problem with Texas A&M was that the coaches were talking about redshirting Thurman, which meant that he would not be able to play football his first year at the school. Thurman wanted to play right away. Oklahoma State University also had a good football program, and Thurman especially liked Jimmy Johnson, the Oklahoma State coach, who now coaches for the

Thurman Thomas (center) poses with Oklahoma State coach, Jimmy Johnson (left), and Oklahoma State star player, Ernest Anderson (right).

When Thomas graduated Willowridge High School June 1, 1984, he was still looking forward to playing for Jimmy Johnson at Oklahoma State.

Dallas Cowboys. Thurman thought often of the day Coach Johnson sat in Thurman's living room and talked about how much he hated to lose. Thurman understood exactly what Johnson was saying because Thurman had that same competitive fire. Thurman really related to Coach Johnson. Also, the coach assured Thurman of two things. One, he would be a running back. And two, he would not be redshirted. In other words, he would get to play his first year.

Thurman took a trip to Stillwater, Oklahoma, to see the Oklahoma State campus and the practice facilities. He instantly fell in love with the place. When he returned home the next day, he told his mother that he had decided to go to Oklahoma State.

"You're not gonna change your mind?" his mother asked.

"Nope. I'm definitely going to Oklahoma State," Thurman said.

Thurman's mother became very sad because her son was moving more than 500 miles away from home.

"Mamma, don't look like that," Thurman said. "You can come up to the games. It'll be all right."[4]

Chapter 4

The Right Choice

Thurman loaded up his car with all his clothes and sports equipment for the drive to Oklahoma State University. His car was a 1984 red Toyota, a brand-new one given to Thurman by his parents for Christmas.

Thurman remembered the day he got the car. He had been in a bad mood Christmas Day because there were no presents under the tree for him. He stayed in his room all morning, and when his mother came to the bedroom door, Thurman said, "You didn't get me anything. I'm not coming out." Thurman didn't know that his parents had bought a car for him a month earlier and were keeping it at his aunt's house until Christmas Day. Now the car was outside in the driveway. Thurman's mother kept insisting that she got him a present, and finally Thurman came downstairs and said, "OK, where's my gift?" She looked at him with a big smile and threw him a set of car keys. He caught the keys and stared at them. His mouth fell wide open. He ran to the window, looked outside, and saw the car. It was his car.

"His eyes lit up like a Christmas tree, he was so happy," his mother, Terlisha, said. "We cut the white bow and ribbon off the car and he got dressed and called his friends. He took them for a ride and they were gone all day."[1]

Thurman and his mom, Terlisha Cockrell.

Now Thurman would be driving to Oklahoma State, where he would play football. He was excited about being in college, but he also was very disappointed that Coach Johnson would not be there as expected. Two months after Thurman signed a letter of intent and agreed to attend Oklahoma State, Jimmy Johnson resigned as coach of Oklahoma State to become coach at the University of Miami. At first, this change angered Thurman so much that he didn't want to go to Oklahoma State. Coach Quinlan at Willowridge High told Thurman that he should call the NCAA to see if he could change his mind and enroll in a different college. Thurman's parents had other ideas, though. The family held a special conference in the living room with Thurman and told him that since he had agreed to attend Oklahoma State, it was like signing a contract. He had an obligation to go. So, like it or not, Thurman was headed for Stillwater, where he would play football for the Oklahoma State Cowboys.

Oklahoma State's new coach was Pat Jones, and Thurman knew very little about him. He wondered if Coach Jones would let him play in the games right away as Coach Johnson had promised. OSU's top running back was All-American Ernest Anderson, who had led the nation in rushing a year earlier. To

Thurman's surprise, however, he was sent into the game often to give Ernest a breather. Thurman did his best, but running against college players from the rugged Big Eight Conference just wasn't as easy as playing high school football. For most of the season, Thurman simply didn't want to embarrass himself.

Adjusting to university life was difficult as well. Thurman would call home and tell his parents that he wasn't happy. It was too cold in Oklahoma, he said. He didn't have many friends. His classes were difficult, and he was worried about not getting passing grades.

"I want to come back home, Mamma," Thurman would say.

"You picked the school, Thurman," his mother would answer. "It must be the right choice."[2]

Late in the football season, Thurman got his first break. Ernest Anderson suffered an injury, and Coach Jones decided to start Thurman at running back for the last few games. Thurman held his own and finished the season rushing for 843 yards. He helped lead his team to the Gator Bowl in Florida. In that game, in front of a national television audience, Thurman carried 32 times for 155 yards and scored a touchdown. He also took a pitchout on a trick play and, with the defense converging on him, stepped up and threw a pass into the end zone to a wide-open receiver for another touchdown. The Cowboys went on to beat South Carolina 21–14, and Thurman was selected as the game's Most Valuable Player. More important, he had the confidence now to play college football. He began preparing right away for his sophomore year by lifting weights to get bigger and stronger.

By the start of his sophomore year, Thurman had gone from 180 pounds to 195. Ernest Anderson had graduated, and Thurman was following in Ernest's footsteps in more ways than one. Like Thurman, Ernest was from southeast Texas and weighed only 180 pounds when he arrived at Oklahoma State. "I really followed Ernest Anderson's career," Thurman said. "He was like me. He was from the [Houston] area and everyone said he was too small. Through his hard work, he gained weight and became a great running back. He was kind of a guiding light for me."[3]

Coach Jones said the comparisons between the two running backs are accurate except for one thing. "Thurman had so many more skills when he got here," Jones said. "Ernest became a great player because of his hard work. He had to make himself into an excellent running back. Thurman was already a great player when he got here. The first time I saw him, I thought what a great player we've found. Now, I just look at him in disbelief because of how much better he gets every day."[4]

The 1985 season began, and Thurman was a hit from the start. The first game was in Seattle, Washington, against the powerful Washington Huskies. Most people figured Oklahoma State had little chance of winning. When OSU quarterback Ronnie Williams went down with an injury, those chances looked even worse. Coach Jones announced to his offensive team on the sideline: "If we're going to win, we're going to have to do it with Thurman."[5] For the rest of the game, the Cowboys just handed the ball to Thurman. It worked. Thurman carried a record 40 times and rushed for 237 yards and a touchdown as Oklahoma State stunned the Huskies, 31–17. Thurman was named the Big Eight Player of the Week. More important, he sent a message that OSU was a team to be reckoned with.

He gained over 200 yards in two more games as Oklahoma State compiled an 8–1 record heading into a showdown with its rival, mighty Oklahoma. The Sooners had the best defense in the nation, and it looked as though Thurman finally would be overmatched. The game was played in a heavy snowstorm, which made it almost impossible to run, but Thurman managed to gain 100 yards on 23

Thomas began his sophomore year with a bang. With his 40 carries and 237 yards rushing, the Cowboys defeated the powerful Washington Huskies.

carries. OSU lost, but Thurman became the only runner to rush for 100 yards against the Sooners, who would go through the season undefeated and win the national championship.

Thurman was the workhorse of the Cowboys' offense all season and finished with 327 carries for 1,650 yards—third best in the nation behind Michigan State's Lorenzo White, who now plays for the Houston Oilers, and Auburn's Bo Jackson who

Thurman put all he had into each game at Oklahoma State.

would win the Heisman Trophy that year before playing football with the Los Angeles Raiders and baseball with the Kansas City Royals. Thurman finished third among underclassmen in the Heisman Trophy voting and would be a nationally recognized player going into his junior year.

Oklahoma State scored 33 touchdowns that season, of which Thurman rushed for 15, returned a punt for another, and passed for two more.

"I have become a different type of back than I was in high school," Thurman said after the season. "I had to. I want to be in for every play. I want to carry the ball every play. To do that, in this league, you have to be ready to take quite a pounding. I have to be able to take the punishment. I didn't think my body would last. But it surprised me. I was a heckuva lot more durable than I thought."[6]

Coach Jones said before the 1986 season began that Thurman would not get as many carries as he did the previous year because other Oklahoma State offensive players who were injured would now be ready to play. "I don't think that will diminish Thurman's productivity," Jones said. "He'll get the yards on less carries. I've just come to expect that of him."[7]

What Jones and the rest of the Cowboys didn't expect was Thurman's getting hurt. Playing with his buddies in a pickup basketball game just before the football season began, Thurman landed awkwardly and twisted his left knee. He was taken to the hospital and received some bad news. There was a torn ligament in the knee, and Thurman needed an operation. He underwent arthroscopic surgery, and it remained to be seen whether Thurman would be able to run as well on that knee after the surgery.

When the season began, Thurman wore a blue knee brace over his left knee. The brace protected his knee, and he never reinjured it. He nicknamed the brace "Old Reliable." Coach Jones thought it was wise to let Thurman's knee heal properly and not overwork it, so he sent in replacement running backs for Thurman every so often. One of the substitutes was Barry Sanders, who would take over at tailback after Thurman graduated and who would win the Heisman Trophy at Oklahoma State. Thurman still led the team in rushing his junior year with 173 carries for 741 yards. It was a year, though, that Thurman wanted to forget as quickly as possible.

When the 1987 season began, it was obvious to opponents that the old Thurman Thomas was back. He cut back and forth, slipping tackles and faking out defenders, just the way he did in his sophomore year. He led his team to its third bowl game in four years by gaining 1,613 yards in 251 carries and scoring a personal best 17 touchdowns.

Thurman also became a celebrity in the Stillwater area, and he often visited children. "I grew up around the YMCA and a lot of people would come and talk to us," Thurman said. "So, in Stillwater, I did a lot of talking for the community. I went to the YMCA's and hospitals and talked to abused kids and stuff like that."[8]

The Sun Bowl was played in El Paso, Texas, on Christmas morning, and Thurman's family was there to see him play his last game for Oklahoma State against the West Virginia Mountaineers. Thurman gave the Cowboys a 6–0 lead in the first quarter on a five-yard run, and the extra point made it 7–0. When West Virginia tied it at 7–7, Thurman came right back to score again from nine yards out to give his team a 13–7 lead. After the extra point it was 14–7. Suddenly, it began to snow, and Thurman wondered if it would affect his running. The Mountaineers scored 17 straight points to take a 24–14 lead at the half, but Thurman wasn't worried. "We weren't going to let 10 points bother us," he said. "We were down by 10 at the half against Missouri this year, too, but we came back to win. We knew we could do it."[9] Thurman was right. He scored two more touchdowns in the

FACT

Thurman missed much of his junior year at Oklahoma State because of a knee injury, and he has worn a blue brace he calls "Old Reliable" ever since. Despite not playing in several games in 1986, and sharing time with teammate Barry Sanders in 1987, Thurman is the school's all-time leading rusher with 898 carries for 4,595 yards. He also is the Cowboys' all-time leader in total yardage, and even completed four of five passes—all for touchdowns.

Thurman Thomas finished his college career as Oklahoma State's all-time leading rusher.

second half and set three Sun Bowl records as Oklahoma State won, 35–33. Thurman finished the game with 157 yards and was awarded the Most Valuable Player trophy.

"The snow didn't affect me at all," he said. "I changed shoes—from a flat surface to just a turf shoe—as soon as it started snowing."[10]

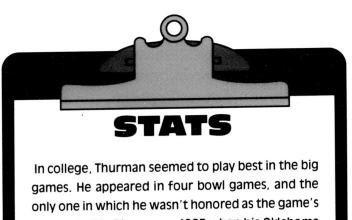

STATS

In college, Thurman seemed to play best in the big games. He appeared in four bowl games, and the only one in which he wasn't honored as the game's Most Valuable Player was 1985 when his Oklahoma State team lost. Here are Thurman's bowl MVP performances:

YEAR	BOWL	CARRIES	YDS	TD	RESULT
1984	Gator	32	155	1	OSU 21, South Carolina 14
1987	Sun	33	157	4	OSU 35, West Virginia 33
1988	Senior	16	97	0	North 21, South 7

West Virginia coach Don Nehlen and the Mountaineers had never played against Thurman before and were very impressed with his running ability. "Thomas is a great, great back,"[11] the coach said after the game.

Thurman was honored as an All-America running back and was picked to play in the Senior Bowl in Mobile, Alabama. It would be his final college game, and he wanted to do especially well because there would be a lot of players in the game who would be playing in the pros the following season. Thurman played for the North, and he led his side to a 21–7 win by rushing for 97 yards on 16 carries. No other running back carried for even half that total, and Thurman was an easy choice for Most Valuable Player.

It was a great finish to a marvelous college career. Thurman knew the next time he put on a uniform, it would be for an NFL team.

Thurman finished as Oklahoma State's all-time leading rusher with 4,847 yards, and the school honored Thurman one last time by retiring his number 34 jersey. That number will never again be worn at Oklahoma State.

Pro coaches and scouts began showing up at the Oklahoma State practice field a few weeks later to check out Thurman. They brought stopwatches and timed his speed. They watched him make cuts,

FACT

Thurman had such a brilliant career at Oklahoma State that the school officially retired his No. 34 jersey during halftime of a basketball game while Thurman was still a senior. OSU has retired only one other jersey number in the history of the school, No. 43 worn by tailback Terry Miller in the mid 1970s, many of whose records Thurman broke.

right and left, to see if his knee was fine. They watched game films of him and talked with Coach Jones about his attitude. The coaches and scouts were quite pleased with what they learned. Los Angeles Rams' coach John Robinson spent two days on campus and said he was excited about drafting Thurman. Other coaches and scouts also said that they wanted Thurman on their team. The Bills' running backs coach Elijah Pitts scouted eight college running backs and returned to Buffalo saying Thurman was the one he liked best. Most of

For the third time in four years, Oklahoma State was going to a bowl game. Thomas's quick moves helped get them there.

the experts were saying on television that Thurman probably would be the first running back taken in the draft. Thurman didn't care which team drafted him as long as he was picked early. It would be an honor to be the first runner chosen.

Two months later, the NFL draft was held and sports fans across the country watched on television. Thurman's family gathered at his apartment in Stillwater, and an ESPN camera crew was set up in his living room to televise the moment he was selected. The draft began, and soon it became the Rams' pick. They selected a running back—but not Thurman. The Rams picked Gaston Green of UCLA. Thurman and his family were surprised because Coach Robinson had said that he wanted Thurman on his team. Soon, another running back was chosen—John Stephens of Northwest Louisiana to the New England Patriots. Then another—Lorenzo White of Michigan State to the Houston Oilers; and another—Brad Muster of Stanford to the Chicago Bears. Thurman was shocked. He was embarrassed. He didn't know what to say. He just sat in his chair, with the television camera on him. His mother began crying and was taken to another room to lie down. Then, another running back was chosen—Craig "Ironhead" Heyward to the New Orleans Saints. A few picks later, still another running back was picked—Ickey Woods of UNLV to the

Cincinnati Bengals. Now Thurman was angry. He knew he was better than these other running backs. He just knew it. Why didn't anybody want him? He decided right then that he was going to prove to all these teams that they made a mistake. Another running back was picked—Tony Jeffery of Texas Christian University to the Phoenix Cardinals. It was obvious that the NFL coaches were concerned about

FACT

Despite his achievements at Oklahoma State, Thurman was only the eighth running back selected in the 1988 NFL draft. The runners chosen ahead of him and the pro teams that drafted them:

1.	Gaston Green	Rams
2.	John Stephens	Patriots
3.	Lorenzo White	Oilers
4.	Brad Muster	Bears
5.	Craig Hayward	Saints
6.	Ickey Woods	Bengals
7.	Tony Jeffery	Cardinals
8.	THURMAN THOMAS	Bills

Thurman's knee, the one he injured while playing basketball. Thurman thought this was so foolish, but there was nothing he could do now.[12]

Finally, it was the Bills' pick in the second round. They made the announcement: "With the 40th pick in the NFL draft, the Buffalo Bills select Thurman Thomas, running back, Oklahoma State." Suddenly, all Thurman's frustration disappeared. He was thrilled to be going to an up-and-coming team like the Bills, and even more than that, he was relieved to have finally been picked. It would be cold in Buffalo, New York, but Thurman didn't care one bit. The family embraced, and Thurman's mother shouted, "It looks like I have to get a heavier coat."[13]

Chapter 5

Something to Prove

Thurman Thomas sat quietly in the corner of the locker room. His eyes were closed. He was breathing very slowly. His stomach was tight, like a huge knot. There were other people, other football players, all around him talking and laughing and getting suited up in their blue and white uniforms. He wanted to open his eyes and talk with them, but his mouth was too dry to speak. Thurman was about to play in his first National Football League game.

Thurman's teammates recognized his discomfort. They had been rookies, too, and knew what it felt like to fear the first game. They walked over to him, a few at a time, and gave him encouragement. "Just think of it as another game,"[1] they said.

Thurman slowly came back to life. He opened

Thurman shows his concentration as he races downfield.

his eyes and began looking nervously around the room. This was it. This is what he had always dreamed of. He looked down at his blue jersey, number 34, his favorite number. He realized he had to snap out of it. Not only was he on the Buffalo Bills, but he was also the starting tailback.

The game was at Rich Stadium in Buffalo, New York, against the Minnesota Vikings. Thurman was happy he wasn't playing on the road in front of a hostile crowd; but on the other hand, over 70,000 fans would be at the Bills' stadium expecting him to do well. What if he wasn't good enough? What if he fumbled? He tried his best not to worry. He knew that doing so would make it worse.

The game began, and the Bills eventually drove down the Vikings' five-yard line. Quarterback Jim Kelly called for a handoff to Thomas. Thurman took the ball and ran toward the hole on the right. He blasted through two defenders, and all of a sudden he realized he was in the end zone. Touchdown. Thurman had become the first rookie to score a touchdown in 1988. It also turned out to be Buffalo's only touchdown of the game.

With less than two minutes remaining, the Bills were clinging to a 13–10 lead. It was second down and seven yards to go. Kelly called the play—a sweep to Thomas. Thurman took the handoff and ran left. He got a block by tight end Butch Rolle and sprinted down the sideline for 28 yards. The Bills had the first down they needed, and they ran out the clock to win the game. Thurman finished with 86 yards rushing on 18 carries. Afterward, he was ecstatic.

"First of all, I didn't really expect to be in there at that time because I was a rookie and it was late in the game. I thought they would put a veteran in like Ronnie [Harmon] or Robb [Riddick]. But when I first went back in there, I figured the coach must have a lot of confidence in me. I was looking to get the first down, and especially to hold onto the football. As soon as I made the first down and was tackled, I got up and three or four of our linemen just grabbed me and I realized that I had just made a very big play in the ball game."[2]

Riddick ran only once in short yardage, and Harmon was used only as a kickoff returner. Bills' coach Marv Levy explained why Thomas was his new starter, even though he was just a rookie. "We have seen a lot of good signs in him," Levy said. "We were pleased. We wouldn't have put him in the game at the beginning if we didn't think he was a player with ability, but you don't find out until now."[3]

The Vikings were impressed with this new Bills'

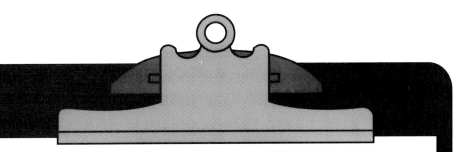

STATS

Thurman runs well when the pressure is on and it shows against rival AFC East foes. Thomas has rushed for 100 yards or more 29 times in five seasons, and more than half of those games have been against AFC East teams:

DATE	OPPONENT	ATT	TOTAL YDS	AVG YDS	LONGEST RUN	TD
10-01-89	Patriots	21	105	5.0	28	1
10-29-89	Dolphins	27	148	5.5	30	1
11-12-89	Colts	29	127	4.4	16	0
9-24-90	Jets	18	214	11.9	60	0
10-28-90	Patriots	22	136	6.2	20	1
11-18-90	Patriots	22	165	7.5	80	2
12-23-90	Dolphins	30	154	5.1	13	1
9-1-91	Dolphins	25	165	6.6	20	1
10-13-91	Colts	20	117	5.9	19	2
11-3-91	Patriots	32	126	3.9	22	1
11-18-91	Dolphins	23	135	5.9	30	1
9-27-92	Patriots	18	120	6.7	31	1
10-26-92	Jets	21	142	6.8	36	0
11-29-92	Patriots	21	102	4.9	16	0
12-6-92	Jets	18	116	6.4	39	0

player, too. "The thing that added a whole new dimension to them offensively was that running back," defensive lineman Henry Thomas said. "He had a good day. No, he had a great day."[4]

It wasn't until after the game that Thurman noticed he had broken the brace he always wears on his left knee. "That right there should tell y'all how good the knee is,"[5] Thurman said. He knew he was just the eighth running back chosen in the draft because people were fearful that his knee might get reinjured. Thurman was determined to prove right away that a lot of teams made a mistake by passing him up.

As the season wore on, Thurman continued to run well as the team's starting tailback. He gained 116 yards against the Green Bay Packers, and then, at Seattle in the tenth game of the season, it all came together for him. "That was the turning point," Thomas said. "That's when I got it all down, felt comfortable with the offensive line and the blocking scheme, had the confidence, felt I could cut back at any time and could just about do anything."[6] Unfortunately, in the Seattle game, the Seahawks' safety Eugene Robinson fell on Thurman's leg, driving his knee brace into his shin. He missed most of that game and the following week against Miami. But he came back strong against Tampa Bay, then had a big game against the Raiders, rushing for 106 yards, including a 37-yard touchdown burst, the Bills' longest scoring run in almost two years.

The Bills won the AFC Eastern Division title with a 12–4 record and beat the Houston Oilers 17–10 in the playoffs with Thurman rushing for 75 yards. Buffalo's season ended the next week in a 21–10 loss to the Cincinnati Bengals in the AFC Championship Game. After the season, the Bills knew they had their running back of the future.

"Basically, he's a pretty confident guy, but with

Thurman takes off, while his teammates keep the New England Patriots in check.

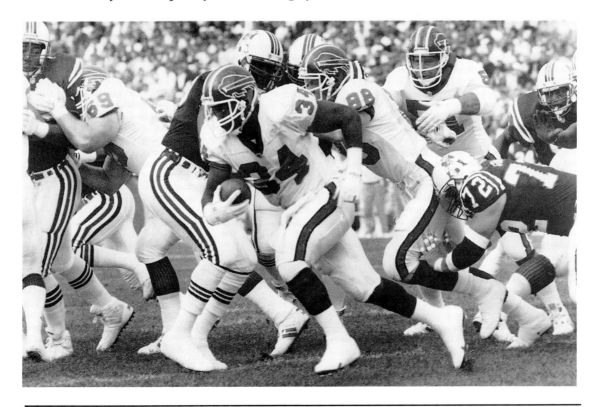

the right amount of rookie humility," Coach Levy said. "He's confident, without a lot of bravado. But, deep down, you could see he believed in his abilities."[7]

Thurman said he had proven that too many teams overlooked him on draft day. "I feel a sense of satisfaction, I really do," Thurman said. "It will always be a thought in my mind that I should have been picked earlier."[8]

Thurman became a premier running back in his second season with the Bills in 1989. He gained over 100 yards rushing against the Patriots, Rams, Dolphins, Colts, and Bengals and became recognized as a complete back and a dangerous weapon because of his receiving skills. He set a new team record for receptions by a running back with 60 catches. He also finished third in the AFC in rushing with 1,244 yards behind Christian Okoye of the Chiefs and Eric Dickerson of the Colts, and tied with Okoye for most touchdowns with 12. He was named to several All-Pro teams and was selected for the Pro Bowl. Thurman wasn't quite satisfied, however. After losing to the Bengals in the playoffs the year before, he wanted to get to the Super Bowl this time.

The Bills traveled to Cleveland for a divisional playoff game against the high-scoring Browns, and it was in this game that Thurman showcased his catching ability. The Browns scored twice on touchdown passes from quarterback Bernie Kosar to receiver Webster Slaughter and got a third touchdown on a 90-yard run by rookie Eric Metcalf. The Bills trailed 34–24 with four minutes left when Kelly tossed a three-yard pass to Thomas in the end zone. Kicker Scott Norwood missed the extra point, leaving the score at 34–30 and requiring the Bills to score another touchdown to win.

The Bills took over again at their 26-yard line with 2:41 left and they drove upfield, converting a crucial fourth and 10 with a 17-yard pass from Kelly to wide receiver Don Beebe. The clock ran down as Buffalo drove to another first down at the 22, then another at the 11, where they had time for two more plays. The first was a pass to Ronnie Harmon in the corner of the end zone. Harmon broke free of the coverage, and Kelly threw the ball perfectly. It came down softly in Harmon's hands . . . and then went right through them. The Bills were distraught over Harmon's drop, but they had to concentrate. Time for one more play. In the huddle, Kelly called "92 F Post." On the pass play, Harmon angled toward the goal posts, Beebe ran a down-and-in, and Thomas drifted to the center of the field. Kelly looked to his favorite receiver—Thomas. Thurman had already made an incredible playoff record-tying 13 catches for 150 yards and two touchdowns. On this play, though, the Browns were expecting a pass to Thomas. Kelly's pass was slightly underthrown and Cleveland linebacker Clay Matthews stepped in front of Thurman to make the interception. Matthews sagged to the turf clutching the football, and the Bills had lost in the playoffs again before reaching the Super Bowl. That wouldn't happen again.

Chapter 6

Super Bowl XXVI

The Bills decided that the 1990 season was going to be different. Anything less than a Super Bowl appearance would be considered by the players as a season of failure. Losing two straight years in the playoffs in games they thought they should have won was very frustrating, and they decided they weren't about to let it happen again. The first step was to finish with the best record in the AFC and gain the home-field advantage throughout the playoffs so they wouldn't have to play on the road.

Thurman Thomas came out blazing by rushing for a personal record of 214 yards on the road against the Jets in a Monday night game. The Bills came out with four wide receivers to spread out the defense, providing the blockers with good angles to open huge holes that allowed Thurman to get into the Jets' secondary. "We running backs

The 2,000-Yard Club

In 1991, Thurman became the 11th player to join the "2,000-yard Club" which combines total yards rushing and receiving. Then, in 1992, Thurman placed his name on the list for a second time:

PLAYER	TEAM	YEAR	RUSH.	RECV.	TOTAL
Marcus Allen	Raiders	1985	1,759	555	2,314
Eric Dickerson	Rams	1984	2,105	139	2,244
O.J. Simpson	Bills	1975	1,817	426	2,243
James Wilder	Buccaneers	1984	1,544	685	2,229
Eric Dickerson	Rams	1983	1,808	404	2,212
William Andrews	Falcons	1983	1,567	609	2,176
Jim Brown	Browns	1963	1,863	268	2,131
Walter Payton	Bears	1977	1,852	269	2,121
THURMAN THOMAS	Bills	1992	1,487	626	2,113
O.J. Simpson	Bills	1973	2,003	70	2,073
Roger Craig	49ers	1985	1,050	1,016	2,066
Walter Payton	Bears	1984	1,684	368	2,052
THURMAN THOMAS	Bills	1991	1,407	631	2,038
William Andrews	Falcons	1981	1,301	735	2,036
Roger Craig	49ers	1988	1,502	534	2,036
Eric Dickerson	Colts	1988	1,659	377	2,036
Walter Payton	Bears	1985	1,551	483	2,034
Walter Payton	Bears	1983	1,421	607	2,028
Eric Dickerson	Rams	1986	1,821	205	2,026
Hershel Walker	Cowboys	1988	1,514	505	2,019
Wilbert Montgomery	Eagles	1979	1,512	494	2,006

think it's to our advantage to get into the secondary," Thomas said after the game. "Then it's one-on-one, and you think no one player is going to bring you down."[1]

Thurman continued his ground assault with 136 yards rushing against the Patriots, 112 against the Cardinals, and 165 against the Patriots. With one game left in the regular season, the Bills and Dolphins were tied with 12-3 records and were playing each other in Buffalo to decide the

Thurman flying over the top of the New York Jets.

Eastern Division title and home-field advantage. Thurman pounded the Dolphins for 154 yards as the Bills triumphed. Two weeks later, in the first round of the playoffs, the Bills faced the Dolphins again, and Thurman carried a career-high 32 times for 117 yards and two touchdowns and caught three passes for 38 more yards as the Bills won,

Marv Levy, coach of the Buffalo Bills.

44–34, in a snowstorm. In the AFC Championship Game the following week against the Raiders, Thurman and the Bills dominated from the start. At the half, they took a commanding 41–3 lead. Buffalo went on to win the game, 51–3, as Thomas gained 138 yards in 25 carries and caught five passes for 61 more.

Thurman created more offensive fireworks in Super Bowl XXV against the New York Giants. The Bills wound up losing, though, 20–19, in the closest Super Bowl in history as they missed a long field goal with three seconds left.

Thurman and his teammates thought he should have been named the Super Bowl's Most Valuable Player. When he showed up for the first game of the 1991 season, he had "Super Bowl XXV MVP" written on his socks.

Soon the Bills would be in another Super Bowl. Thurman opened the season with 165 yards rushing against Miami, then surpassed the 100-yard mark against the Steelers, Bears, Colts, Patriots, Packers, Dolphins again, and finally the Jets. He finished the season with his highest rushing total yet: 1,407 yards. He was third in the NFL in rushing behind Emmitt Smith of the Cowboys and Detroit's Barry Sanders, Thurman's old teammate at Oklahoma State. Thurman had

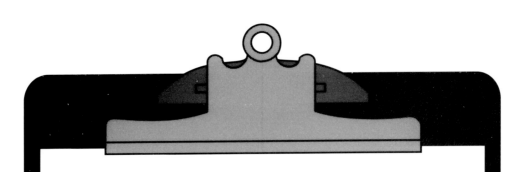

STATS

Thurman became the first player in NFL history to lead the league in total yards from scrimmage for four consecutive years, breaking the mark of legendary running back Jim Brown. Detroit Lions running back Barry Sanders, Thurman's teammate at Oklahoma State, is often compared to Thurman. Here is a comparison of their years in the pros:

YEAR	PLAYER	RUSHING YARDS	RECEIVING YARDS	TOTAL YARDS
1989	Thomas	1,244	669	1,913
	Sanders	1,470	282	1,752
1990	Thomas	1,297	532	1,829
	Sanders	1,304	462	1,766
1991	Thomas	1,407	631	2,038
	Sanders	1,548	307	1,855
1992	Thomas	1,487	626	2,113
	Sanders	1,352	225	1,577

missed the rushing title in 1990 by seven yards and thought he would get it this time. But the Bills had clinched home-field advantage for the playoffs and didn't need him down the stretch, so he played just one quarter in the final two games of the regular season. Still, he led the NFL in total yards rushing and receiving for the third straight year, tying the feat of the legendary Jim Brown. For that, he was chosen as the NFL Player of the Year.

Before the Bills' first playoff game against the Chiefs, NBC announcers Bill Parcells and O.J. Simpson, the former Buffalo great, were seated in the press box. Parcells looked at the Wall of Fame at Rich Stadium and told Simpson, "They're going to take down your name and put up Thurman Thomas."[2] Parcells was kidding, but certainly Thurman's name will one day go up next to Simpson's.

Against the Chiefs, Thurman rushed 22 times for 100 yards in leading his side to victory once again. In the AFC final the following week, Denver held Thomas to 72 yards on 26 carries, but the Bills managed to knock Broncos quarterback John Elway out of the game and win, 10–7. The Bills had earned their second straight trip to the Super Bowl. They never expected anything less.

The Bills would be playing the champions from the NFC—the Washington Redskins—at the

Metrodome in Minneapolis, Minnesota. Thurman and the Bills couldn't wait to get another chance at winning it all. After the game, maybe they wished they had picked another day, or at least another opponent. The Redskins pounded the Bills throughout the game and eventually won, 37–24, after a gallant Bills' comeback fell short.

For Thurman, the game was a nightmare from the start. First, he couldn't find his helmet. The Bills began their first offensive series while Thurman searched along the bench for his helmet. "For some reason, somebody moved it," Thomas said. "I don't know why. It was just one of those situations where everybody was running around. I was very upset."[3] When Kelly turned to hand off to Thomas on the game's first play, he was surprised to find himself giving the ball to backup Kenneth Davis instead. "I was wondering what was going on," Kelly said.[4] Thomas found his helmet and got into the game on the third play, but the Bills couldn't gain a first down and had to punt. Even though Thurman missed only the first two plays, the case of the "missing helmet" would become the most remembered incident of Super Bowl XXVI.

The Washington offense took the field, and the Redskins were on fire from the start. They scored two touchdowns and a field goal in the first half to lead 17–0, and just 16 seconds into the third quarter, they scored again to move ahead 24–0. The Bills had no choice but to pass on every down from then on. Kelly set a Super Bowl record with 58 passes, but Thurman's running threat was effectively removed from the game, and he finished with just 13 yards on 10 carries. While the Redskins' offense was scoring, the defense was harrassing Kelly with four interceptions, five sacks, three fumbles, and ten passes knocked down.

Afterward, the Bills were more than disappointed in the locker room—they were embarrassed. "I told you before the game that we'd go out and make history," defensive end Bruce Smith said. "We did, but in the wrong way."[5]

Thurman spent the next hour answering the same question over and over again to different reporters: "Thurman, what happened to your helmet?" It certainly wasn't something the star running back wanted to be remembered for in a Super Bowl game. The Bills returned home to Buffalo. Before parting company, they announced as a team that they must return once again to the Super Bowl to make up for the heartbreaking loss to the Giants and the embarrassing loss to the Redskins. Sure enough, they would get yet another opportunity.

Chapter 7

One More Time

The 1992–93 regular season was a race for first place in the AFC East between the Bills and the Miami Dolphins, who added free agent tight end Keith Jackson to their potent passing attack. Quarterback Dan Marino led the Dolphins to an early-season victory in Buffalo, a convincing 37–10 win that sent a message to the Bills that they weren't the only good team in the AFC East.

In a Monday night game three weeks later, the Bills were on the verge of falling two games behind in the standings. They trailed the New York Jets, 20–17, with less than two minutes left in the game at the New Jersey Meadowlands. The Jets had just scored on a short touchdown run. Thomas was having a terrific game running the ball for the Bills. As Buffalo took possession at its own 25-yard line there wasn't enough time to keep the ball on the ground. Quarterback Jim Kelly swiftly moved the team downfield with passes of 34 and 19 yards to receiver Don Beebe. Thurman ran once on the drive—a huge 18-yard gain to the Jets' 12-yard line that put Buffalo in position to score. It gave Thurman 142 rushing yards for the night, easily the best performance by any player on the field. With just 51 seconds left, Kelly called for pass play. His favorite target in the clutch has always been Thurman, and this time was no different. Kelly dropped back and zipped a pass to Thurman who caught it between two defenders in the end zone for a 24–20 victory. Thurman had opened the season with a four-touchdown performance at home against the Rams in a 40–7 triumph. This win over the Jets, though, was even more satisfying.

The Bills and Dolphins met in a rematch in week 10. They were tied for first place with 7-2 records. The winner would take a one-game lead in the division race as the playoffs drew near. Marino completed his first 11 passes as the Dolphins took an early 14–3 lead to the thrill of the hometown fans. The Bills answered with a field goal and then a touchdown that was set up when Kelly connected with Thurman on a 26-yard pass play. Buffalo took a 20–17 lead in the third quarter and then got two more field goals to move ahead, 26–17. Miami needed a touchdown and a field goal to win, and they got the field goal with four minutes left in the game. With Miami's high-powered offense on the sideline waiting for one last chance, it was up to the Buffalo offense to keep the ball. The Bills burned as much off the clock as they could but found themselves in a third and four situation with just over a minute left. Miami was out of time-outs, so if the Bills could convert the first down, they would win. Kelly knew who his clutch player was and called for a handoff to Thurman. Thomas ducked through a small hole in the middle of the line and then leaped past a defender to get the first down by a yard. "I've never had a bigger run," Thurman told reporters afterward. "Not in junior high, high school, college or the pros."[1]

Thurman rushed for over 100 yards in five of the last six games of the season, but the Bills won only three of the six games. The Dolphins went on to win the AFC East. Once again, Buffalo had made the playoffs, but only as a wild card entry, which meant that the Bills would have to play two games on the road in the playoffs if they could make it that far. By now, though, the Bills were playoff veterans, and they weren't intimidated by road games. After the first half of

FACT

If Thurman rushes for 100 yards or more, the Bills usually win. When Thomas gained 102 yards at Indianapolis on November 29, 1992 and the Bills lost, 16–13, it snapped a streak of 25 straight wins by the Bills when Thurman eclipsed the 100-yard mark. Strangely, Thurman rushed for 116 yards the following week against the Jets and the Bills lost *again*, this time 24–17. Still, Buffalo is 27–2 overall when Thurman gains 100 yards or more in a game.

the opening round wild-card game in Buffalo, however, it didn't look as though the Bills would get the chance to play on the road.

Buffalo trailed the Houston Oilers 28–3 at halftime, and the offense was without its quarterback as Kelly was injured early in the game and had to use crutches to walk. The Bills knew Frank Reich was a good backup quarterback, but Reich didn't show it when one of his first passes in the second half was intercepted by Cris Dishman

Thomas supports his teammates, even when he is off the field.

and returned for another Oilers' touchdown. Houston led the game 35–3 early in the third quarter. Everyone assumed that the game was over. Everyone, that is, except Thurman Thomas and the Bills. Reich rallied the Bills in the second half to the most stirring playoff comeback in history as his side scored touchdown after touchdown. The Oilers' defense could do nothing to stop the awesome Bills' offense, and Buffalo finally tied the game, 38–38, to force overtime. Houston began the fifth period with the ball, but on the third play, Warren Moon was intercepted deep in Houston territory. The Buffalo offense ran two safe handoff plays and then sent in kicker Steve Christie who made the winning field goal. The fans in Rich Stadium erupted with joy as the Buffalo players celebrated wildly. It appeared that the Bills were destined for the Super Bowl once again.

The following week, Buffalo traveled to Pittsburgh to take on the tough Steelers, the champions of the AFC Central. Without Kelly to direct the offense, the Bills knew they had to run the ball with Thomas, who finished the regular season as the AFC's second-leading rusher. The problem was that Thurman was suffering from a nagging hip injury, and it hurt each time he got tackled. Plus, the Steelers knew Thurman would be getting the ball, and they were waiting for him. Thomas

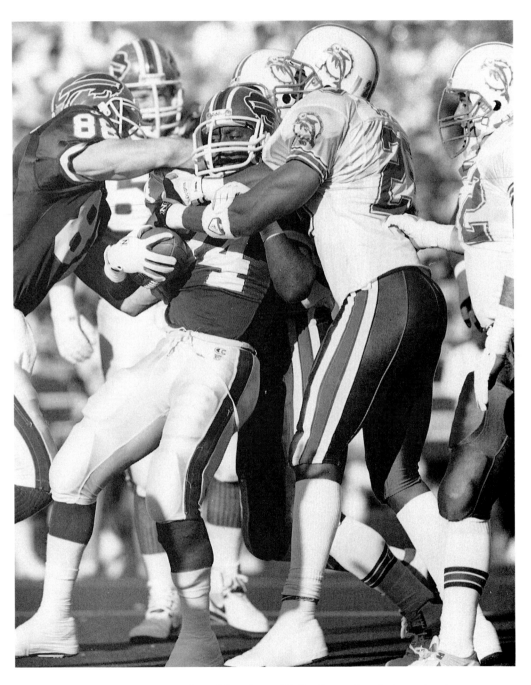

Thomas's teammate Pete Metzelaars (#88) tries to break the grip of Miami defensive back Louis Oliver.

carried the ball 19 times, but the Steelers held him to 54 yards. Without their starting quarterback and with Thomas bottled up, the pressure was on the Buffalo defense. Defensive end Bruce Smith, linebackers Cornelius Bennett and Shane Conlan, and the rest of the defense knew it had to play at a higher level for the Bills to have a chance. The Steelers took an early 3–0 lead, but could not score again the rest of the day. The Bills scored touchdowns in the second, third, and fourth quarters and cruised to a 24–3 victory. Meanwhile, in Miami, the Dolphins were hammering the San Diego Chargers 31–0, setting up another showdown between the Dolphins and Bills—with the winner headed for the Super Bowl.

Thurman's hip was still bothering him when he jogged onto the field the following Sunday in Miami for the AFC title game. He had made up his mind in the locker room, though, that he wasn't going to let it slow him down as it did the previous weekend in Pittsburgh. "This is the type of game," Thomas said the day before the Miami game, "that the great player steps it up to a higher level."[2] Thurman did just that. He ran the ball through the Miami defense all day, gaining 96 yards on 20 carries and catching five passes for 70 more yards, including a 17-yard touchdown. The Bills drilled the Dolphins, 29–10. "My role is basically to get the offense going," Thurman said after the game. "I think I showed that. When I'm healthy, I can go in and get the job done and move the team up and down the field."[3] The Bills were on their way to Pasadena to meet the Dallas Cowboys in Super Bowl XXVII. It would be Buffalo's third straight trip to "The Show."

Thurman knew exactly what to expect from reporters during the two weeks leading up to Super Bowl XXVII. "With all the records and the yardage," he said, "the number one question will be, 'What happened to your helmet?'" Thurman was prepared to explain how he had placed his helmet at the end of the Bills' bench before the start of Super Bowl XXVI against the Redskins, only to find that someone had moved it. He knew that missing the first two plays of the game while searching for his helmet did not affect the outcome of the game, but he also knew that reporters would need to find stories to write about—and the "missing helmet" story would be a popular one. So Thurman was ready. He listened to the same question, over and over, day after day, for a week. Finally, a few days before the game, Thurman showed up at a press conference with a bag of 100 miniature helmets with the Bills' logo on the sides. He gave every reporter a little Bills' helmet. "Hold onto this helmet," Thurman told each reporter with a smile. "Let's see if you can keep from losing your helmet before Sunday."[4]

The Cowboys cruised through the playoffs by pounding the Philadelphia Eagles, 34–10, and then beating the San Francisco 49ers on the road, 30–20. Dallas would be the third straight NFC East foe to meet the Bills in the Super Bowl, following the Giants and the Redskins. Most observers figured the Cowboys were probably the best of the three. This would be a special game for Thurman for another reason. Dallas was coached by Jimmy Johnson—the coach who had recruited him to Oklahoma State. Thurman remembered how Coach Johnson left Oklahoma State two weeks later to coach at the University of Miami. "If we win, it could be a great payback," Thomas said. "When he recruited me, he guaranteed that he would be there for four years, and then two weeks later he took the job at Miami."[5]

Buffalo coach Marv Levy said the day before the game that turnovers were the key to victory. "There's only one ball," Levy said. "We've got to keep it, and they've got to take it away."[6]

The game started well for Buffalo when Steve Tasker blocked a Dallas punt out of bounds at the 16-yard line and the Bills scored four plays later as

Thurman ran two yards into the end zone for a touchdown. The extra point was good, and the Bills had a 7–0 lead. Unfortunately, Thurman sprained his ankle on the touchdown run, and it would affect him the rest of the game.

The Bills got the ball back again and were in

STATS

Hall-of-Fame running back O.J. Simpson has long been considered the Bills' greatest player ever. Now Thurman has overtaken "The Juice" in several categories. Thurman is fast closing in on O.J.'s most impressive record of all—career yards. Here's a comparison of the two greats:

Rushing				
PLAYER	ATT	YARDS	AVG	TD
Simpson	2,123	10,183	4.8	57
Thomas	1,376	6,316	4.6	35

Receiving			
PLAYER	REC	YARDS	TD
Simpson	175	1,924	12
Thomas	247	2,666	16

control as they drove to midfield. Then, suddenly, everything changed. Quarterback Jim Kelly threw a wobbly pass intended for tight end Pete Metzelaars that was intercepted by Dallas safety James Washington. The Cowboys scored in six plays on a 23-yard pass from quarterback Troy Aikman to tight end Jay Novacek. Dallas took a 14–7 lead moments later when Kelly fumbled the ball near his goal line. It was grabbed out of the air by Dallas lineman Jimmie Jones, who stepped into the end zone for a touchdown. It was a big defensive play by the Cowboys, who would make an even bigger one a few minutes later. The Bills sped down the field to the Dallas four-yard line on their next drive, but three running plays left them a yard short of the touchdown. On fourth down, Kelly rolled to his right and tried to pass the ball to Thurman, but he was covered. Kelly desperately threw the ball into a crowd, and it was intercepted by Thomas Everett. It was Kelly's third turnover in seven minutes, and it would be his last. On the Bills' next series, blitzing Dallas linebacker Ken Norton, Jr. crashed into Kelly's knee and knocked him out of the game. Backup Frank Reich came in, just as he had a month earlier in the miracle comeback against the Oilers. Could Reich direct another comeback? For a few minutes, it appeared he

Jim Kelly was knocked out of the game by Dallas linebacker Ken Norton, Jr.

might. Reich drove the Bills 61 yards to the Dallas six-yard line, where Steve Christie kicked a field goal to cut the Dallas lead to 14–10.

The Cowboys came right back as Aikman, threw a 19-yard touchdown pass to Michael Irvin. The Cowboys took total control moments later because of a crucial mistake by Thurman. On Buffalo's first play from scrimmage, with less than two minutes left in the half, the Bills called a swing pass to Thomas. Thurman caught the ball and sidestepped Jimmie Jones at the 17-yard line, cut back, and was stripped of the ball by the long right arm of defensive end Leon Lett. Jones, who chased Thomas, fell on the ball. Dallas scored on the next play as Aikman threw an 18-yard touchdown pass to Irvin. Suddenly, it was 28–10 at the half. "Actually, I was trying to make a big play out of something," Thurman explained afterward. "I had faked a couple of guys out, and one of the guys I faked out came back and just stripped me."[7]

The Cowboys kicked a field goal to move ahead 31–10 midway through the third quarter, but the Bills came back as Reich hit wide receiver Don Beebe for a 40-yard touchdown on the final play of the quarter. Dallas took control from that point, scoring three touchdowns in the fourth quarter to win the game, 52–17. Thomas finished the game with just 10 carries for 19 yards and four catches for 10 yards. "I guess their defensive scheme was designed to stop Thurman, and if you have 11 guys trying to stop one person, you're not going to have a good game," Thurman said in the locker room. "Anytime you have nine turnovers, you're not going to win any football game. It's hard to get over this one. The loss to the Giants was heartbreaking. This one was embarrassing."[8]

Still, the Bills remain one of the premier teams in the NFL and will likely be in the playoffs and making a charge at the Super Bowl for several

FACT

The Bills are just the second team in NFL history to play in the Super Bowl three years in a row. The Miami Dolphins appeared three straight times in the early 1970s. Although the Bills didn't win the "Big Game" during the streak, the Dolphins—led by coach Don Shula—won twice.

VI	Dallas Cowboys 24, Miami Dolphins 3
VII	Miami Dolphins 14, Washington Redskins 7
VIII	Miami Dolphins 24, Minnesota Vikings 7
XXV	New York Giants 20, Buffalo Bills 19
XXVI	Washington Redskins 37, Buffalo Bills 24
XXVII	Dallas Cowboys 52, Buffalo Bills 17

Thurman Thomas: Star running back.

years to come—especially with Thurman Thomas in the backfield.

"Thurman has gained a lot of respect from his teammates because he's tough—he carries his load," Coach Levy says. "Thurman has the No. 1 quality all the great running backs have: balance. He has the ability to dart and feel the hole, and he knows when to accelerate a little bit. He has that innate feeling—like a kid in a schoolyard—of knowing when to dodge."[9]

Thurman Thomas can trace his success back to his childhood, back to the days on Roberson Street, where his father and uncle taught him to dart and feel the hole, and when to dodge. He also learned one final thing from his parents, and he says it is this lesson that has allowed him to become one of the greatest players in the NFL.

"Don't get involved in drugs. Hang around the right crowd," Thurman says of his biggest lesson. "Ever since my parents told me that when I was little, I always hung around the right club and never got involved in fights. I stayed away from rough neighborhoods. You have to use common sense when you are out there. If you see trouble is getting ready to start, you walk away from it."[10] Or, as Thurman does so well, you run away from it. Fast.

Notes by Chapter

Chapter 1

1. George Diaz, "Bills Didn't Lose Because of Thomas," *Orlando Sentinal* (Janurary 28, 1991), p. D9.

2. Dan Dierdorf, Super Bowl, ABC.

3. Al Michaels, Super Bowl, ABC.

4. Frank Gifford, Super Bowl, ABC.

5. Clark Judge, "Giants Scuttle the No-huddle," *San Diego Tribune* (January 28, 1991), p. D-1.

6. Judge.

7. Judge.

8. George Diaz, "Bills Didn't Lose Because of Thomas," *Orlando Sentinal* (January 28, 1991), p. D9.

9. Diaz.

Chapter 2

1. Interview with Terlisha Cockrell, (January 20, 1993).

2. Ibid.

3. Ibid.

4. Ibid.

Chapter 3

1. Interview with Neal Quinlan, (December 18, 1992).

2. Ibid.

3. Ibid.

4. Interview with Terlisha Cockrell, (January 20, 1993).

Chapter 4

1. Interview with Terlisha Cockrell, (January 20, 1993).

2. Ibid.

3. John Klein, "OSU's Thomas stands tall in early Heisman picture," *Houston Post* (August 10, 1986), p. C12-C13

4. Ibid.

5. Ibid.

6. Ibid.

7. Ibid.

8. Mark Meighen, "Thomas Transforms from Rookie to Veteran," *GameDay Magazine* (October 9, 1988), p. 6-7.

9. Bill Knight, "Thomas, sophomore linebacker win awards," *El Paso Times* (Dec. 26, 1987), p. 1

10. Ibid.

11. Ibid.

12. Interview with Terlisha Cockrell, (January 20, 1993).

13. Interview with Terlisha Cockrell, (January 20, 1993).

Chapter 5

1. Mark Meighen, "Thomas Transforms from Rookie to Veteran," *GameDay Magazine* (October 9, 1988), p. 6-7.

2. Ibid.

3. *Football Digest* (July/Augst 1991), pp. 17-21.

4. Milt Northrop, "Thomas Lives Up to Expectations," *Bills' Notebook* (September).

5. Northrop.

6. Michael Knisley, "Advantage Thomas," *The Sporting News* (December 23, 1991), p. 12-13.

7. Donn Esmonde, "There's No Doubting Thomas Now," *Buffalo News* (December 13, 1988), p. D1.

8. Esmonde.

Chapter 6

1. *Football Digest* (July/Augst 1991), pp. 17-21.

2. Robert F. Schranz, "Thurmanator," *Buffalo Bills Magazine* (December 22, 1991), p. 29.

3. Clark Judge, "Washington Gets Super Win," *San Diego Tribune* (January 27, 1992), p. D1.

4. Tom Cushman, "Bills Helped Buffalo Themselves," *San Diego Tribune* (January 27, 1992), p. D1.

5. Ibid.

Chapter 7

1. Associated Press, "Bills Cash in on Miami Mistakes, Claim First Place," *San Diego Union-Tribune* (November 17, 1992), p. C2.

2. Clark Judge, "Matchups," *San Diego Union-Tribune* (January 17, 1993), p. C6.

3. Clark Judge, "Buffalo Back Again, Makes It Look Easy," *San Diego Union-Tribune* (January 18, 1993), p. D1.

4. Don Norcross, "Super Bowl Notebook" *San Diego Union-Tribune* (January 29, 1993), p. C10.

5. Associated Press, "Cowboys, Bills Check Rose Bowl," *San Diego Union-Tribune* (January 31, 1993), p. C7.

6. Jerry Magee, "Hurry-up Bills or Pokes? It's Time to Settle It," *San Diego Union-Tribune* (January 31, 1993), p. C1.

7. Clark Judge, "Thomas Adds a New Chapter to His Personal Super Bowl Follies," *San Diego Union-Tribune* (February 1, 1993), p. D17.

8. Judge.

9. *Football Digest* (July/August 1991), pp. 17-21.

10. Mark Meighen, "Thomas Transforms from Rookie to Veteran," *GameDay Magazine* (October 9, 1988), p. 6-7.

Career Statistics

YEAR	TEAM	RUSHING					RECEIVING		
		G	ATT	YDS	AVG	TD	REC	YDS	TD
1988	Bills	15	207	881	4.3	2	18	208	0
1989	Bills	16	298	1,244	4.2	6	60	669	6
1990	Bills	16	271	1,297	4.8	11	49	532	2
1991	Bills	15	288	1,407	4.9	7	62	631	5
1992	Bills	16	312	1,487	4.8	9	58	626	3
TOTALS		78	1,376	6,316	4.6	35	247	2,666	16

Where to Write Thurman Thomas

Mr. Thurman Thomas
c/o Buffalo Bills
1 Bills Drive
Orchard Park, NY 14127

Index